Wonders of the World

Everglades

The Largest Marsh in the United States

Nancy Furstinger

www.av2books.com

AV² provides enriched content that supplements and complements this book. Weigl's AV² books strive to create inspired learning and engage young minds in a total learning experience.

Your AV² Media Enhanced books come alive with...

Audio
Listen to sections of the book read aloud.

Video
Watch informative video clips.

Embedded Weblinks
Gain additional information for research.

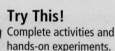

Try This!
Complete activities and hands-on experiments.

Key Words
Study vocabulary, and complete a matching word activity.

Quizzes
Test your knowledge.

Slide Show
View images and captions, and prepare a presentation.

... and much, much more!

Go to **www.av2books.com**, and enter this book's unique code.

BOOK CODE

W318043

AV² by Weigl brings you media enhanced books that support active learning.

Published by AV² by Weigl
350 5th Avenue, 59th Floor
New York, NY 10118
Website: www.av2books.com   www.weigl.com

Library of Congress Cataloging-in-Publication Data

Furstinger, Nancy.
The Everglades / Nancy Furstinger.
    p. cm. — (Wonders of the world)
Includes index.
ISBN 978-1-62127-473-5 (hardcover : alk. paper) — ISBN 978-1-62127-479-7 (softcover : alk. paper)
 1. Everglades National Park (Fla.)—Juvenile literature. 2. Natural history–Florida–Everglades National Park–Juvenile literature. I. Title.
F317.E9F86 2013
508.759'39—dc23

                                2012040447

Printed in the United States of America in North Mankato, Minnesota
1 2 3 4 5 6 7 8 9 17 16 15 14 13

112012
WEP301112

Editor Heather Kissock
Design Mandy Christiansen

Every reasonable effort has been made to trace ownership and to obtain permission to reprint copyright material. The publishers would be pleased to have any errors or omissions brought to their attention so that they may be corrected in subsequent printings.

Photo Credits
Weigl acknowledges Getty Images as its primary photo supplier for this title.

Contents

A River of Grass

Imagine a river of grass teeming with wildlife. This watery wilderness is the Everglades. It is the largest **marsh** in the United States. Everglades National Park was the first national park dedicated to protect wildlife. It is the only **subtropical** preserve in North America and the only everglade in the world.

The Everglades began to form at the end of the last **Ice Age**, about 10,000 years ago. As the ice melted, a shallow sea flooded the southern part of Florida.

Today, the Everglades is a popular place for tourists to visit. If visitors are lucky, they might spot a rare **species**, such as the Florida panther or the West Indian manatee.

The Everglades is home to more than 1,000 different species of plants.

The diversity of bird species found in the Everglades attracts bird watchers from around the world.

Everglades Facts

- The Everglades includes 5,000 square miles (13,000 square kilometers) of land and water—about the same size as the state of Connecticut.

- The Everglades is the only place in the world where alligators and crocodiles exist together.

- Everglades National Park is the largest national park east of the Rocky Mountains.

- Everglades National Park has been named a World Heritage Site, an International Biosphere Reserve, and a Wetland of International Importance.

- More than 350 species of birds have been identified within the park.

Map of Florida

•Orlando

ATLANTIC OCEAN

•Tampa

St. Petersburg•

GULF OF MEXICO

•West Palm Beach

Florida

•Fort Lauderdale

•Miami

LEGEND

Water

The Everglades

• City

N

0 _____ 62.5 miles

0 _____ 62.5 km

The Pa-Hay-Okee boardwalk provides excellent views of the Everglades. The boardwalk's name comes from a American Indian term meaning "grassy water."

The paper wasp is common to the Everglades area. It can be identified by the orange color on its antennae, wings, and legs.

A Trip Back in Time

An ancient sea covered the southern Florida peninsula 6 million years ago. The remains of plants and animals on the sea floor slowly turned into limestone. This formed the bedrock of the Everglades. This porous rock is called "egg-stone" because it looks like tiny fish eggs.

Glaciers did not reach southern Florida during the last Ice Age. As the melting ice returned to the sea, however, it helped shape the Everglades. The land was covered by the water from the melting ice four times. Each time the land was covered, more rocks formed.

One of the most colorful birds of the Everglades is the purple gallinule, sometimes called a sultana or water hen.

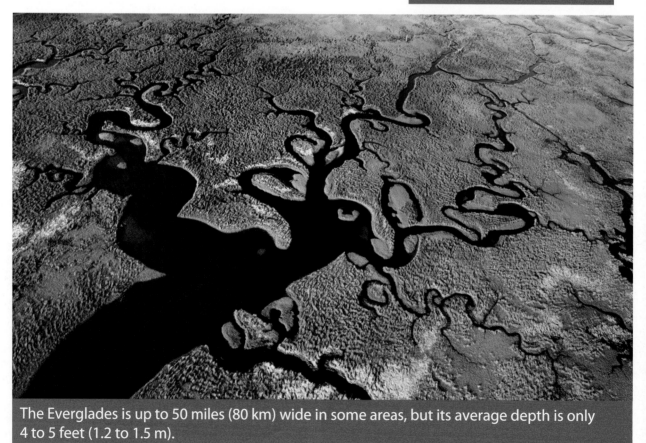

The Everglades is up to 50 miles (80 km) wide in some areas, but its average depth is only 4 to 5 feet (1.2 to 1.5 m).

Puzzler

Salt water borders much of the Everglades, affecting the community of plants and animals living in southern Florida.

Q: Saltwater bodies of water surround most of the United States. Can you identify the bodies of water in the map below?

HINT: Most of the islands in the world are found in this ocean.

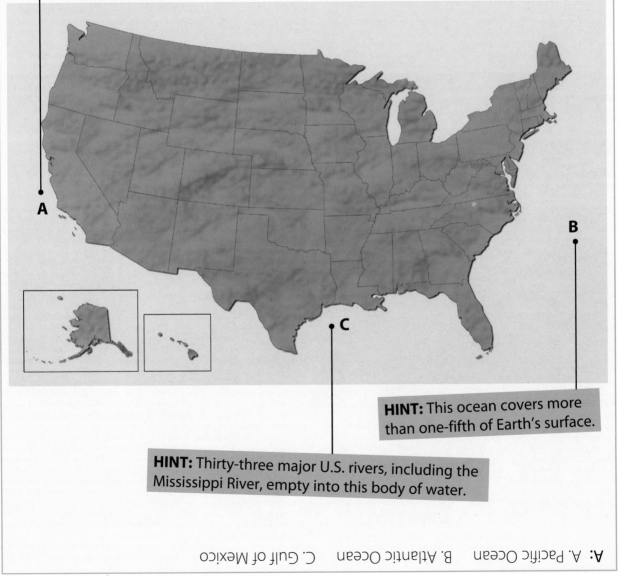

A

B

C

HINT: This ocean covers more than one-fifth of Earth's surface.

HINT: Thirty-three major U.S. rivers, including the Mississippi River, empty into this body of water.

A: A. Pacific Ocean   B. Atlantic Ocean   C. Gulf of Mexico

Changing the Flow

For thousands of years, the overflow from Lake Okeechobee has supplied the Everglades with fresh water. Wide but shallow, the Everglades becomes salty as it nears Florida Bay and the Gulf of Mexico. Humans have altered the course of this water flow with more than 1,400 miles (2,250 km) of **canals** and **levees**.

During the rainy season—May through September—thunderstorms may dump 12 inches (30 cm) of rain on the Everglades in a single day. Humid summer temperatures can reach 90° Fahrenheit (32° Celsius). The hurricane season runs from June through November. December through April is the dry season. Winter temperatures may dip as low as 53°F (12°C).

Although humanmade canals help make the Everglades more accessible to people, they also cause damage by changing natural water levels in the area.

River of Sand

Lake Okeechobee is the third largest freshwater lake located entirely in the United States. It is a remnant of the prehistoric Pamlico Sea.

An underground river of sand is found above Lake Okeechobee. It extends south under the Everglades and Florida Bay. This sand deposit was worn away from the Appalachian Mountains 3 to 5 million years ago. The sand, called the Long Key Formation, holds fresh water.

Hundreds of keys, or small islands, dot the Florida Bay. These tiny islands formed in the shallow bay waters, which average only 4 to 5 feet (1.2 to 1.5 metres) deep. Mangrove roots grow in the mud beneath the murky water. **Silt**, trapped among the roots, collects and forms new land.

Everglades Ecosystems

An ecosystem is a community of plants and animals that interacts with its environment. An ecosystem can be as small as a rotting log or as large as an ocean. The community of plants and animals found in the Everglades is affected by the natural changes in this large marsh.

Water has a major effect on life in the Everglades. Plants and animals have adapted to the wet and dry cycles. During the rainy season, the river of **sea grass** turns muddy and then flows.

When the rains cease, water levels drop and the dry season begins. The swampy areas attract snakes, frogs, and turtles. These animals are part of the food chain for alligators, crocodiles, and nesting wading birds.

The American alligator is usually between 6 and 12 feet (1.8 and 3.7 m) long, but can grow up to 19 feet (5.8 m) in length. American alligators live for about 50 years in nature.

Habitats of the Everglades

A variety of unique **habitats** can be found within the Everglades' boundaries. A few of them are listed below.

Florida Bay In Florida Bay, keys and sea grass shelter green sea turtles, schools of fish, hammerhead sharks, and seahorses.

Mangrove Forests Where fresh water meets salt water, mangrove forests help pink shrimp spawn and house nesting birds.

Coastal Prairie Inland, on the coastal prairie, desert plants withstand waves and wind.

Fresh Water Teardrop-shaped tree islands called hammocks grow in freshwater **sloughs**. White-tailed deer munch on nutrient-rich sea grass.

Swamps Cypress trees grow out of swamps, offering havens for pelicans and roseate spoonbills.

A Park in Danger

In 1934, a special committee convinced Congress to create Everglades National Park. The park would protect endangered birds and safeguard the freshwater and saltwater habitats. When the park was finally created in 1947, President Harry S. Truman said, "The spectacular plant and animal life distinguishes this place from all others in our country."

Today, the Everglades is considered one of the country's most endangered national parks. Mercury from air pollution gets into the water and poisons the water, fish, and all the animals that depend on fish for their diets. Sea grass is dying off in Florida Bay. These problems are connected to human development. Pollution and a change in the water flow are some of the problems affecting the Everglades.

WARNING
HEALTH HAZARD
DO NOT EAT MORE THAN ONE BASS PER WEEK PER ADULT DUE TO HIGH MERCURY CONTENT
CHILDREN & PREGNANT WOMEN SHOULD NOT EAT BASS
NPS-EVER

Mercury can be very harmful if consumed by humans. The National Park Service posts signs and puts warnings on its website to alert visitors when high levels of mercury have been detected in Everglades fish.

What Can I Do?

There is no other place in the world like the Everglades. Although it is a protected national park, this does not guarantee the survival of endangered species. Humans have changed the Everglades. Land development, pollution, and changing water flow—all of these activities cause problems for animals. Wherever you live, you can do your part to help.

Conserve water. Do not waste water by letting it run while you wash your hands or brush your teeth. Take short showers instead of baths.

Spread the word by informing your friends about what they can do to help.

When visiting parks, do not feed animals. Never attempt to turn them into pets. Do not pick plants or remove natural objects from parks. Stay on the park trails and avoid making loud noises.

Stop pollution. Never throw trash on the ground or in the water.

Animals on the Brink

Fifteen endangered species call Everglades National Park home. Animals in danger of becoming extinct include the 1,000-pound (454-kilogram) West Indian manatee, or sea cow. These gentle creatures rest just below the water, where they risk being hit by speeding boats.

The American crocodile roams mangrove swamps, eating fish. This reptile's habitat is threatened by human development. The long-legged wood stork is in danger because of water control programs. On land, the Florida panther is fighting for survival. Its habitat is being destroyed. This large brown cat is also at risk of being killed by cars and other vehicles.

More manatees are killed worldwide by human activity than by any other cause. In Florida, crashing into canal gates and colliding with motorboats are the two leading causes for manatee deaths.

Biography

Ernest Coe (1866–1951)

As a boy, Ernest Coe enjoyed exploring the outdoors in New Haven, Connecticut. As a landscape architect in Miami, Florida, Coe used plants and trees to decorate gardens and other public and private spaces. When he realized that rare birds in the Everglades were being killed by poachers, Coe discovered a new mission. He vowed to preserve the Everglades. Coe created the Tropical Everglades National Park Association in 1928. His efforts spurred interest in the new Everglades park. Nicknamed "Father of the Everglades," Coe loved the tropical beauty of the region.

The Big Picture

The world can be divided into biomes. Biomes are major natural communities that share similar climates, plants, and animals. One biome is wetlands, such as marshes, swamps, and bogs. Wetlands are a natural link between earth and water. Whether salty or fresh, wetlands filter pollution out of water and prevent floods. This map shows some of the world's best-known wetland areas.

Everglades
United States

NORTH AMERICA

ATLAN
OCE

EQUATOR

PACIFIC
OCEAN

SOUTH
AMERICA

Pantanal
Brazil, Bolivia, Paraguay

SOUTHERN
OCEAN

LEGEND

- Wetlands
- Ocean
- River

Scale at Equator

0   1,000   2,000   3,000 miles

0   1,000   2,000   3,000 km

N

ARCTIC OCEAN

ASIA

The Fens
United Kingdom

EUROPE

Western Siberian Lowland
Russia

AFRICA

EQUATOR

INDIAN
OCEAN

AUSTRALIA

Congo River Basin
West-Central Africa

SOUTHERN
OCEAN

ANTARCTICA

People of the Everglades

Paleo-Indians once hunted bison and mammoths in the Everglades region around 10,000 BC. When the wetlands emerged after the climate changed, they began to catch shellfish.

When the Spanish arrived in the early 1500s, about 20,000 American Indians lived in southern Florida. By 1763, when the English gained control of Florida, the area's American Indian population had shrunk to several hundred. Warfare, slavery, and European diseases, such as smallpox, reduced the American Indian population.

The Seminoles were one of several groups who lived in the Everglades. They lived in "chickees," which are open-sided houses with thatched roofs.

Puzzler

Early Aboriginal Peoples of the Everglades found the resources they needed in nature. They fashioned sharks' teeth into knives and used shells to make fishhooks, picks, hammers, and chisels.

Q. Why were shells and sharks' teeth the most practical materials for making tools?

A: The Aboriginal Peoples of the Everglades could find these materials nearby.

Everglades Timeline

Prehistoric

65 million years ago Dinosaurs become extinct.

6 million years ago A shallow sea covers Big Cypress Swamp in southern Florida.

5 million–3 million years ago Sands worn away from the Appalachian Mountains are deposited along the Florida peninsula.

1 million years ago Glaciers form on all continents; rocks form beneath the Everglades.

100,000 years ago The sea level in southern Florida rises 100 feet (30 m) above modern levels. Billions of tiny coral animals begin forming the Florida Keys.

10,000–8,000 years ago Paleo-Indians live in the area, adapting to new wetlands.

5,000 years ago Cypress swamps and hardwood forests begin developing.

8,000 BC–750 BC Early peoples in wetlands who rely on shellfish create tools and pottery.

Exploration

AD 1500–AD 1750 The first Europeans reach the Everglades.

1763 The English gain control of Florida from Spain.

1817–1858 During three Seminole Wars, American Indians travel to the Everglades to avoid being removed from Florida.

Development

1880s Developers begin digging drainage canals.

1905–1910 Areas of wetlands are transformed into farmland.

1928 Ernest Coe creates the Tropical Everglades National Park Association.

1947 President Harry S. Truman dedicates Everglades National Park.

1948 Congress authorizes the Central and South Florida Project. Roads, canals, levees, and water-control structures are built.

1976 Everglades National Park becomes an International Biosphere Reserve and a World Heritage Site.

1987 Everglades National Park becomes a Wetland of International Importance.

1989 The Everglades Expansion Act adds East Everglades to the park.

Present

2000 Congress passes the Everglades Restoration Plan as part of its Water Resources Development Act.

2012 The Florida State government commits $880 million to cleaning up and restoring the Everglades.

Water Conflicts

The natural resources of the Everglades face many challenges. Water is at the heart of the problem. Florida's growing population and tourists must share water from the Everglades with endangered wildlife. Since the 1920s, humans have changed the natural flow of water into the park. Canals, pumps, and dikes send water to farms and **urban** areas first. Only then can water be used by the plants and animals living in the Everglades. In 2000, the government began a 30-year plan to restore the Everglades. The Comprehensive Everglades Restoration Plan involves removing levees and canals to help restore the natural flow of the river of grass.

In September 2012, the Florida State government committed $880 million to further restoration projects in the Everglades. These projects are to include creating shallow water basins for water storage and expanding upon the network of humanmade marshes already in the area. Creating more marshland is expected to reduce the amount of **pollutants** flowing into the Everglades.

Some farmers in the Everglades have water brought in by trucks to irrigate their crops.

Should engineers have altered the flow of water in the Everglades?

Yes	No
About 1,000 people requiring 150,000 gallons (568,000 liters) of fresh water daily move to Florida every day. In addition, 85 million tourists vacationing in Florida make demands on water supplies. There were not enough freshwater sources to supply this demand. It was believed that water from the Everglades should be used.	It is dangerous when people try to control water flow by changing wet and dry seasons. Releasing too much water flooded alligator nests, destroying eggs. Wood storks could not locate enough fish to breed and feed young. Cattail replaced sea grass. Withholding too little water reduced the number of apple snails. As a result, river otters and Everglade kite birds had less to eat.
Water in the Everglades needed to be controlled to help farmers. The wetlands were drained and used for farming and ranching. Fresh water was provided for sugarcane and vegetable fields, citrus farms, dairy farms, and cattle ranches.	When fresh water runs low, salt water invades the wetlands, upsetting the balance of nature. Runoff from farming fertilizer and chemicals harms the environment, causing problems for Everglades plants and animals.

Natural Attractions

There are countless ways to enjoy the vast beauty of the Everglades. The following are samples of things to see and do.

At Billie Swamp Safari, you can study snakes or watch alligator wrestling. Hop aboard a swamp buggy and head to Sam Jones Camp, where you will learn about the medicine man who led Seminole resisters. Then, sample local food specialties at the Swamp Water Café. Try eating gator nuggets, frog legs, catfish, and fry bread with honey.

Explore the weaving waterways of the Ten Thousand Islands, where the Everglades meet the sea. Park rangers work as guides on boats, pointing out dolphins, manatees, and birds in the maze of mangroves.

"The Everglades is a test. If we pass it, we get to keep the planet," said environmentalist Joe Podger. Your class might be interested in helping this fragile environment by using the park as an outdoor classroom. Each year more than 10,000 students participate in the Everglades National Park's Education Program.

Airboat rides are a popular attraction for visitors to the Everglades. Airboats are designed with a flat bottom and an above-water propeller to avoid getting stuck in shallow or marshy waters.

Be Prepared

If you plan to visit the Everglades, even for just an afternoon, it is important to bring supplies with you. To enjoy a safe outing, stay on the trails and keep a careful distance from all animals.

Do not forget to bring sunglasses, sunscreen, and insect repellent.

Wear a hat and protective long-sleeved clothing.

Bring snacks.

Carry binoculars and a camera.

Bring 3 to 4 quarts (3 to 4 L) of water per person, per day.

A Natural Heritage

Nature has influenced the arts and culture of the Everglades region. Pieces of clay pottery that have been found show early peoples' skill with natural materials. Huge shell mounds mark sites where villages were once located. The early peoples piled up oyster and whelk shells as sites for sacred temples and burial sites.

Today, people continue to be inspired by this river of grass. Seminoles create sweetgrass baskets and palmetto fiber husk dolls to sell at powwows. Nature photographers capture on film the splendor of the Everglades.

The Seminoles make baskets from the wild sweetgrass found in the Everglades basin. The grass is hand-picked, washed, and then laid in the sunlight to dry before being sewn together with colorful thread.

Everglades Mythology

Seminole children have long gathered to listen to campfire legends. In Seminole **mythology**, the Creator, the Grandfather of all things, selected the panther as the first being to walk on Earth. The Creator admired the large cat for its beauty, patience, and strength. He sealed up all of the creatures in a large shell. When the shell cracked, the panther leapt out first. The Creator called the panther Coo-wahchobee, meaning "crawls on four legs close to the ground."

The Creator placed the animals into clans, or groups. Today, Seminoles are members of one of eight clans: Bear, Bigtown, Bird, Deer, Otter, Panther, Snake, and Wind. The Panther clan creates laws and makes medicines.

The Florida panther was one of the first species added to the U.S. Endangered Species list. There are fewer than 100 Florida panthers remaining in the wild today.

True or False?

Decide whether the following statements are true or false. If the statement is false, make it true.

1. During the last Ice Age, a shallow sea flooded the Everglades.

2. The Florida Keys are islands of coral rock.

3. The Everglades has both rainy and dry seasons.

5. The Everglades is not an endangered national park.

6. There are 15 endangered species living in the Everglades.

4. Early Aboriginal Peoples of the Everglades made tools from sharks' teeth.

Short Answer

Answer the following questions using information from the book.

1. Which two animals can only be seen together in the Everglades?

2. When is hurricane season?

3. Who led the fight to preserve the Everglades?

4. What did early Aboriginal Peoples of the Everglades use to make tools?

5. Seminoles believe which animal was the first to walk on Earth?

Multiple Choice

Choose the best answer for the following questions.

1. In which state is Everglades National Park?
   a. Georgia
   b. Alabama
   c. Florida

2. The park was first formed to preserve endangered
   a. birds
   b. alligators
   c. manatees

3. In which year did Ernest Coe create the Tropical Everglades National Park Association?
   a. 1858
   b. 1928
   c. 1934

4. These people moved to the Everglades in the 1800s:
   a. the Spanish
   b. the Paleo-Indians
   c. the Seminoles

Activity

See the Difference

Oceans are known for their salt water. Fresh water, on the other hand, has very little salt. As a result, fresh water weighs less than salt water. The more water weighs, the higher its **density**. Surfaces with high density are better able to carry or hold objects that are less dense. This means that objects should float better in salt water than in fresh water. Follow the steps below to see how salt water differs from fresh water.

Materials

1 fresh egg

Salt

1 large glass

Spoon

Water

Instructions

1. Fill the glass with fresh water. Carefully, add the egg to the glass of fresh water. Watch what happens.

2. Remove the egg from the glass of fresh water.

3. Stir some salt into the glass of water. Carefully, place the egg in the salt water. Watch what happens.

4. Did the egg float better in salt water or fresh water?

Key Words

canals: artificial waterways

density: the state of being closely set

habitats: places where plants or animals live and grow

Ice Age: the last period in Earth's history when glaciers covered large areas of the planet

levees: artificial riverbanks built to prevent flooding

marsh: an area of soft, wet land; a border between land and water

mythology: stories about ancient times or natural events

peninsula: a portion of land surrounded by water on three sides

pollutants: substances that render the air, soil, water, or other natural resource unsuitable for a specific purpose

sea grass: a type of grass that grows 3 to 10 feet (1 to 3 meters) out of the water

silt: fine sand or mud carried by moving water

sloughs: wide, shallow waterways

species: a specific group of plants or animals that shares characteristics

subtropical: a region bordering the tropical zone

urban: related to the city

Index

Log on to www.av2books.com

AV² by Weigl brings you media enhanced books that support active learning. Go to www.av2books.com, and enter the special code found on page 2 of this book. You will gain access to enriched and enhanced content that supplements and complements this book. Content includes video, audio, weblinks, quizzes, a slide show, and activities.

AV² Online Navigation

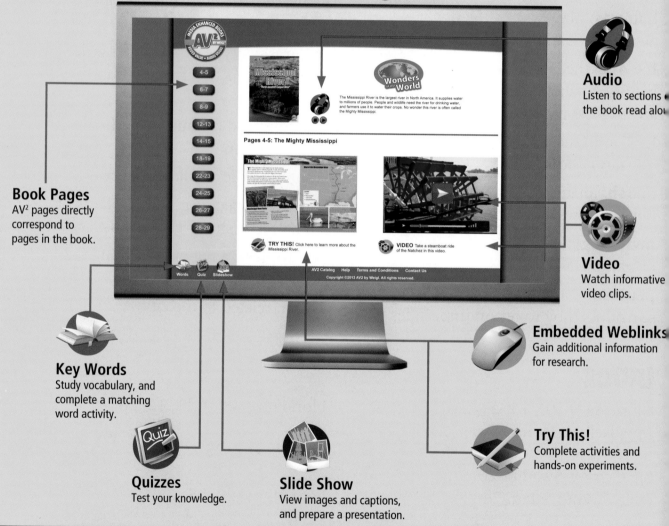

Audio
Listen to sections of the book read aloud.

Video
Watch informative video clips.

Book Pages
AV² pages directly correspond to pages in the book.

Key Words
Study vocabulary, and complete a matching word activity.

Quizzes
Test your knowledge.

Slide Show
View images and captions, and prepare a presentation.

Embedded Weblinks
Gain additional information for research.

Try This!
Complete activities and hands-on experiments.

AV² was built to bridge the gap between print and digital. We encourage you to tell us what you like and what you want to see in the future.

Sign up to be an AV² Ambassador at www.av2books.com/ambassador.